A Guide To Uncontested Divorce In New Jersey

2nd Edition

Bari Zell Weinberger, Esq.

FAMILY LAW REFERENCE COLLECTION
Weinberger Divorce & Family Law Group

Copyright © 2019 Bari Z. Weinberger

All rights reserved. No part of this publication may be reproduced, distributed, or transmitted in any form or by any means, including photocopying, recording, or other electronic or mechanical methods, without the prior written permission of the publisher, except in the case of brief quotations embodied in critical reviews and certain other non-commercial uses permitted by copyright law. For permission requests, write to the publisher, addressed "Attention: Permissions Coordinator," at the address below.

Weinberger Law Group Library
119 Cherry Hill Road, Suite 120
Parsippany, NJ 07054

www.WeinbergerLawGroup.com

ISBN-13: 978-1-942725-18-3

A Guide to Uncontested Divorce In New Jersey

Table of Contents
Letter from the Author 8
Chapter 1: What is Uncontested Divorce? 9
    Understanding the Settlement Process 14
    Settlement Process Step-By-Step 17
    Questions to Ask an Attorney 32
Chapter 2: Tips for Settlement Negotiations 36
    Take Charge of Your Own Case 37
    Begin Settlement Efforts Early 37
    Use Negotiation Tactics Wisely 38
    The Art of Compromise 40
Chapter 3: Marital Settlement Agreements 45
    Legal Effects of the MSA 48
    Amending Your MSA 49
    What To Do If Settlement Efforts Fail 49
Chapter 4: Procedural Requirements 51
    Preparing a Complaint 52
    Deciding the Plaintiff and the Defendant 53
    Residency Requirements 53
    Information to Include in the Complaint 55
    Request for Relief 58
    Serving the Complaint 62
    Responding to a Complaint 63
Chapter 5: Default Judgments 65
    Request for Default 66
    Affidavit of Non-Military Service 66
    Default Hearing 67
    Uncontested Divorce by Default 69
Chapter 6: After Defendant Files an Answer 71

Case Management and Discovery 72
The Case Information Statement 73
Additional Discovery Tools..79
Chapter 7: The Uncontested Divorce Hearing 81
Questions to Expect at the Hearing 82
Potential Post-Judgment Matters 86
Further Information and Resources 88
What To Bring To An Initial Consultation 90
5 Factors That Wreak Havoc On Finances 93
5 Factors That Wreak Havoc On Parenting 95
5 Factors That Wreak Havoc On Future 97
Other Titles in the Series of Family Law Guides..................100

About the Author

Bari Z. Weinberger, Esq. is a certified matrimonial law attorney and founding partner of Weinberger Divorce & Family Law Group of New Jersey. Ms. Weinberger has been named a Top Women in Law by New Jersey Law Journal and carries an AV Preeminent (highest) peer rating from Martindale Hubbell. She recently celebrated 10 years of recognition on the state's SuperLawyers list.

In addition to working with clients at her firm, Weinberger Divorce & Family Law Group, Ms. Weinberger is the Associate Author of the New Jersey Family Law Practice, 15th Ed., a 5-volume treatise utilized by virtually every family law judge and practitioner in the State of New Jersey.

www.WeinbergerLawGroup.com

Disclaimer

This book provides a general overview of New Jersey divorce and family law matters for informational purposes only. The contents included do not in any way supplement or replace legal advice obtained by a qualified and licensed attorney.

The information provided herein is based solely upon my professional experiences in the areas of New Jersey divorce and family law. While every effort has been made to ensure that the information contained in this book is helpful and of high quality, no representations or warranties of any kind are made with regard to the completeness or accuracy of the included content.

Please note that information provided within this guide is current as of publication date. Due to the complexity and frequency with which the divorce and family laws change, you should consult with a qualified attorney to determine the best course of action for your specific legal needs.

If you require legal advice based on the specifics of your case as it relates to New Jersey laws, please feel free to reach out to our office to schedule a consultation with one of our experienced attorneys. It would be our pleasure to help you.

For more information about other topics related to family law, such as alimony, domestic violence, prenuptial agreements, family mediation, child support and child custody, domestic partnerships, or any other family law related topics, please ask us about our other books. All guides in the series are designed, like this one, to help you to make sound decisions regarding your family's individual situation. Please keep in mind, however, that these books contain general information, and not legal advice. Always direct specific questions about your own situation to an attorney.

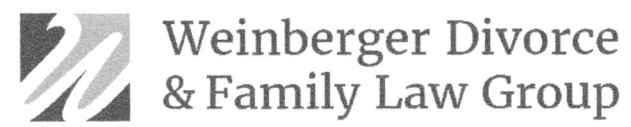

Weinberger Divorce & Family Law Group

Safeguarding Your Future™

Letter from the Author

As a family law attorney, it is my mission to help my clients achieve a settlement in their divorce matter that leaves them feeling confident and satisfied as they move forward into the next chapter of their lives. Throughout the divorce process, I want the individuals I work with to be fully informed, understand that they have choices, and enjoy true peace of mind . . . every step of the way.

In writing this guide to uncontested divorce in New Jersey my goal is to provide relevant, easy-to-understand information that I genuinely hope will empower you to make positive, constructive decisions for you and your family. I also hope to dispel some myths about what an uncontested divorce is, and what it is not. All too often, in the movies, and on TV, divorce is shown as a tension-filled courtroom showdown, with the judge left in charge of deciding such pivotal matters as what happens to a couple's children, or who gets to keep the family fortune.

In reality? In an uncontested divorce, spouses come together in an out-of-court setting to negotiate their own terms, including agreements concerning division of assets, alimony, child support, child custody, and more. When a divorce settlement is mutually agreed upon by both parties, it is then signed and submitted to the court, and the divorce is finalized. A growing number of couples in New Jersey are turning to the process of uncontested divorce because it is generally faster, less expensive and more amicable than the contested route.

As you read through the information here, I encourage you to take notes and stop frequently to reflect on your needs, and how this model might be able to fulfill those needs, or not. For many couples, with appropriate legal guidance and support, it is absolutely possible to achieve a divorce settlement out of court without litigation. For other couples, there may be major disagreements, especially over child-related matters or assets that are best solved by appearing before a judge. My one and only goal is to present you with information that can help you make the best choices possible for you and your family.

For the complete picture of all the many possibilities open to you, I encourage you to read my guide about contested divorce as well. However, I should point out that every divorce situation is unique, so please understand that these guides are not a substitute for personal legal advice.

Most of all what I would like you to know is that you can be in control of your divorce. For many of you reading this, pursuing an uncontested divorce may be the most effective way to get there. If you have any questions about uncontested divorce, or wish to discuss the specifics of your situation, please contact us to set up a free consultation. Together, we can help you determine the best course of action for achieving the settlement you want.

All my best,
    Bari Z. Weinberger

Chapter 1

What is Uncontested Divorce?

All too often, in the movies divorce is shown as a tension-filled courtroom showdown, with the judge left in charge of deciding such pivotal matters as what happens to a couple's children, or who keeps the house. In reality? In an uncontested divorce, spouses come together in an out-of-court setting to negotiate their own terms.

A growing number of couples in New Jersey are turning to the process of uncontested divorce because it is generally faster, less expensive and more amicable than the contested route.

When Sarah and Marco decided that ending their marriage would be the best way for each of them to find happiness in life and be good parents to their three-year-old son, they talked about the divorce process and the kind of time and money it would take to reach a settlement. Neither looked forward to divorce court and to having a judge decide their matter, and the couple also realized, after a few conversations, how few unresolved issues their divorce actually contained. Sarah and Marco both believed that joint physical and legal custody would be best for their son and both understood their responsibilities regarding child support. When it came to their home -- their biggest asset -- there was some tension, but they each seemed open to negotiation.

Do couples like Sarah and Marco need to spend the time and money involved in going before a family court judge to get a decision on their divorce-related issues? In New Jersey, the answer to this question can be no, thanks to the out-of-court settlement process called uncontested divorce.

If you are not familiar with the term, an uncontested divorce can occur in either of two situations:

- You and your spouse have issues to resolve in your divorce, but there are ==no significant disagreements concerning divorce-related issues such as child custody and support, division of marital property, or spousal support, making it==

possible for you to settle your divorce out of court, or

- Your spouse fails to appear or respond to divorce papers, either by choice because he or she believes that this is an effective way to oppose the divorce, or because he or she cannot be located.

This book will focus on the first of these two situations. If you and your spouse have agreed to proceed with an uncontested divorce, or if you have not yet agreed but are hoping to settle all your issues outside of a courtroom, the information in this book will be helpful.

- - - -

FAQ: Can We Get an Uncontested Divorce If We Strongly Disagree Over Some Issues?

If you and your spouse have disagreements that seem insurmountable, this does not necessarily mean that you will be unable to pursue an uncontested divorce. If you are in this situation, this book includes information to help you settle your case. Couples going through a divorce in New Jersey can take steps to resolve their case at any stage, and the great majority of divorce cases settle at some point prior to trial. As a general rule, the earlier you are able to settle, the more you will benefit from bypassing costly and time-consuming court procedures. In some cases, however, settlement will not be possible. If you and your spouse believe that you have exhausted the possibilities for settlement on one or more of your issues and that moving on to a contested (court litigated) divorce option that makes sense, you can refer to our book "A Guide to Contested Divorce in New r to the information on contested divorce the ɜr Divorce & Family Law Group website: http://..... y/contested-divorce.

- - - -

Practical Tip: Is an Uncontested Divorce Right For You?
Before proceeding any further, make a list of issues at stake in your divorce and what you think a fair outcome for each of these issues should be. Think about what your partner has expressed about these issues and compare results. Or, if you are able to, simply ask your spouse how he/she is feeling about support, asset and debt distribution and custody (if applicable). How far apart are your goals? Where do you disagree? This can help you start to understand your options.

> If you and your spouse do not settle your divorce civilly, you will be forced to let a judge – a stranger – determine the matter for you.

Bari Z. Weinberger, Esq.

Understanding the Uncontested Divorce Settlement Process

If you and your spouse have decided to move on to divorce and have unresolved issues that you would like to settle out of court, pay close attention to the following information about the settlement process. Thinking about settling disagreements in divorce, however small or large, can be challenging. There are few situations in life where disputes can carry such a powerful emotional impact. Some people are so resistant to the idea of a marriage ending, or are so angry with their soon-to-be former spouse, that the idea of negotiating with their spouse seems unbearable.

When working through difficult emotional responses, keep in mind that if you and your spouse do not settle your divorce civilly, you will be forced to let a judge—a stranger—determine the matter for you. You will likely spend significant money on legal fees and time out of your everyday life to fight over issues that could possibly be resolved early on in the case. People often fail to grasp the full ramifications of such a prospect. Some people think that it will be better if a judge makes the decisions in their case, possibly because they are convinced of the superiority of their position, or because they believe that a judge will be wise and impartial.

While most judges do indeed strive to be impartial, getting a case before a judge can be extremely expensive. In addition, family law judges tend to be overburdened due to the large number of cases requiring court decisions. A family law judge does not have time to become familiar with the personal details of each case, and for this reason, may not be tuned in to the intricate issues that you think are most important. Judges are human beings who have off days just like anyone else, and judges sometimes have strong personal opinions that may work in a contrary direction to what you believe is an ideal and fair solution. While you might get a favorable result from one judge, you might get a very different result from another, and you cannot select the judge that is assigned to your case.

If you and your spouse have minor children, settlement encompasses an additional dimension. Having a stranger decide major financial matters for you is stressful, but having a stranger dictate the circumstances of your children's lives can be emotionally wrenching. Although unfortunate situations do exist where one or both parents are unwilling or unable to parent effectively, in most families, those best equipped to make decisions about living situations for children are the children's parents. While you and your spouse may have major disagreements about how to parent or where the children should live, it may be likely that your spouse at least cares deeply for your children and wants to see them in a positive situation. A judge will decide matters regarding children based on the child's best interests, but a judge will not have day-to-day knowledge about your child and will not have the kind of emotional attachment that comes from knowing a child since birth or living in the child's household.

- - - -

FAQ: What Are the Benefits of an Uncontested Divorce?

Simply put, court procedures can be expensive and time-consuming, and all too often they increase the conflict and complexity of a divorce. Putting major decisions about

your finances or your family in the hands of a judge is risky and expensive at best. While there are some situations where this result is necessary, it makes sense for most people to try to avoid it. Settling a case outside of a courtroom provides many benefits:
> A. You and your spouse will retain more control over the exact terms of a settlement.
> B. You will be more likely to have terms that are clear and that both of you understand, and
> C. You will avoid the possibility of extended litigation, including re-arguments and appeals, which can sometimes continue for years.

- - - -

Practical Tip: Find Emotional Balance.
Sometimes it's emotions -- your own and/or your spouse's -- standing in the way of reaching an amicable, uncontested resolution to your divorce matter. Some couples think "uncontested divorce" is only for couples who are on relatively good terms with each other. This may be the case in some divorces, but not all. What matters in uncontested divorce is only how "amicable" and civil the two of you are when it comes to settling the legal issues involved in your divorce -- not your personal issues. To be able to keep calm and focused on your matters at hand, however, it may be in your best interest to seek counseling with a qualified mental health counselor or social worker who specializes in helping people going through a divorce. Family counseling or parent-child counseling can also be helpful at this time.

Settlement Process Step-By-Step

Uncontested divorce procedures in the state of New Jersey vary somewhat depending on the circumstances of each case and the rules of the county in which a case is filed. Each county court / vicinage follows state law and state court rules while also establishing its own procedural rules. You can obtain more specific information directly from the court or from an attorney with experience practicing family law in your county. You can also find statutes dealing with divorce, dissolution of civil unions, annulment, and divorce from bed and board in Title 2A, Chapter 34, of the New Jersey Statutes Annotated (N.J.S.A.) The most up to date versions available in searchable unannotated form on-line at the New Jersey Legislature official website: http://bit.ly/NJ-Legislature. Notwithstanding any slight variations from county to county, proceeding through an uncontested route will generally be faster and less expensive than proceeding with a contested case.

The following is a step-by-step overview of what the New Jersey uncontested divorce process generally entails. Additional documentation or steps may be required depending on where you live.

Step One: Know the Facts of Your Situation and Organize your Documents

Although your goal is to settle everything at the earliest opportunity, this does not mean that you can be sloppy and incomplete with documentation. You and your spouse may be planning to attend mediation before filing a complaint, a process in which you work with a mediator to reach a divorce settlement out of court. (See the FAQ later in this chapter for more information about divorce mediation). Even so, it will be important for you to collect all of the financial documents you would need if your case were going to court.

This includes documents providing complete and accurate information about all assets or financial obligations belonging to one or both of you, the current income of each of you (or the potential income, if current income does not reflect earning ability), and a detailed budget covering current and anticipated expenses. You can find a more complete checklist below. The sooner you can put together a complete financial picture, the more efficiently you will be able to proceed. Filling out a New Jersey Family Part Case Information Statement (CIS) (found at the New Jersey Courts official website: http://bit.ly/nj-cis) is a good way to formulate an overview of your financial situation and help you complete an accurate budget.

There is information later in this book that will guide you step-by-step through completion of your CIS (see Chapter 6).

It can be a daunting task to assemble everything you need to fully analyze your financial situation. The most critical documents you will need to get started are those that verify the current income of both you and your spouse, such as tax returns, recent pay stubs, and W-2 forms, as well as copies of any court documents already filed in your case, any papers you have been served with that may require a response, and any premarital or marital agreements between you and your spouse.

You may eventually need to produce documents showing all or most of the following:

Income and Investments for the Past One to Three Years (unless otherwise noted):
- W-2 statements for the past three to five years for you and your spouse,
- Three most recent paystubs from your employer,
- State and federal individual and business income tax returns,
- Monthly bank statements for all joint and individual accounts,
- Monthly statements for all stocks, bonds and mutual funds,
- Any trust documents affecting you, your spouse, or your children,
- Documents showing income on any investment properties, such as rent receipts,
- Account statements for annuities, certificates of deposit, 529 accounts, UTMA/UGMA accounts, or other financial accounts in the name of you, your spouse, or any of your children, and
- Statements for all retirement accounts, including pensions, 401(k)s and 403(b)s, IRAs, SERPs, SEPs, ESOPs, or any other retirement-type accounts.

Property Ownership
- Deeds and purchase documents for your primary residence,
- Deeds and purchase documents for any other real property holdings, including rental properties or vacation homes,
- Ownership documents for any business property owned partially or fully by either you or your spouse, with evidence of percentage ownership,
- Purchase documents or appraisals for any personal property of significant value (antiques, collectables, jewelry, art, furs, etc.),
- Registration certificates or title documents for automobiles or other vehicles, and
- Documents evidencing separate ownership of property by either spouse, including a list of property owned prior to marriage, a list of any purchases made with such property, and any documents evidencing an inheritance by either spouse.

Bills and Outstanding Debt for the Past One to Three Years
- Property tax statements,
- Mortgage statements,
- Credit card statements, whether joint or individual,
- Vehicle or equipment leases,
- Tax liens or notices from the IRS,
- Utility bills,
- Student loan documents or tuition bills,
- Any other loans or notes payable,
- Outstanding medical bills,

- Arrearages on prior spousal or child support orders or agreements, and
- Monthly budget worksheets (Quick Books, Quicken, Case Information Statement).

Legal Documents
- Any documents already filed in court,
- Any court papers you have been served with,
- Wills,
- Living wills,
- Powers of attorney,
- Trust agreements,
- Social Security statements,
- Advance healthcare directives or healthcare proxies,
- Pre-nuptial or post-nuptial agreements,
- Divorce judgments, marital separation agreements, or support orders from any previous marriage,
- Any other lawsuits, judgments, or garnishments, and
- Business partnership agreements and financial records.

Insurance Documents
- Health insurance documents indicating carrier, policy and group numbers, and persons covered,
- Life insurance declaration page indicating carrier, policy number, face amount, cash value, insured, and beneficiaries,
- Auto insurance declaration page indicating carrier, policy number, vehicles covered, insured, and term,

- Homeowner's insurance declaration page indicating carrier, policy number, and residence covered,
- Long-term care insurance declaration page indicating carrier, policy number, and insured, and
- Disability insurance documents indicating carrier, policy number, and insured.

We have included a complete list of necessary financial documents at the end of this book. To help you identify and organize your information, you can print this list out, write in amounts and add your own notes.

Practical Tip: How to Keep Financial Records Organized.
As you prepare for divorce, it can feel like you have amassed a small mountain of financial paperwork. Before things get out of control, take time to become organized by buying an extra-large three-ring binder, a package of clear sheet protectors, and a set of tabbed dividers. In the binder, insert dividers labeled according to the different sections noted above (income & investments, property ownership, etc.). Place each bill or statement in a separate sheet protector and place in its corresponding section. Bring this binder with you to all meetings related to your divorce. If you have access to a printer scanner, scan and make copies of your documents for email communication and document backup.

Step Two: Review Your Goals

The next step in approaching settlement will be to clarify your goals. Consider any issues you believe will exist in your case and ask yourself any of the following questions that might be applicable to your situation:

- **Child custody**: Which parent will serve as the primary residential parent? Will both of you have an equal say in all major matters affecting the children, such as schooling, religion and health? Are you and your spouse likely to agree about these issues?

- **Child support**: Have you accounted for all extracurricular activities and childcare costs (if needed). Do you have a child with special health/medical needs? Conduct a thorough inventory of all costs involved with raising and caring for your child.

- **Visitation plan**: Start thinking about possible options that might work for the whole family. Fill out a blank calendar with your initial scheduling ideas.

- **Marital home**: Who is currently living in the home? Will you or your spouse remain there, and if so, for how long? Will you sell the home, or will one of you buy out the other's interest?

- **Other assets and debt division**: What resolution do you consider reasonable? Are there any assets such as businesses that need to stay with one spouse or the other for practical reasons? If the division of assets will be unbalanced, is this fair? If not, can the balance be equalized in some way?

- **Spousal support / alimony:** Is this likely to be a factor? Does one of you have a much higher income than the other? Has one spouse been financially dependent for an extended period of time?

- **Attorney's fees and expenses:** What will be the source of payment? Are there joint accounts that are able to cover legal fees?

- **Beneficiaries of insurance policies:** Health insurance may be tied to one spouse's employment. Will this change? Will either spouse want to change beneficiaries on life insurance or other policies?

Step Three: Gain Legal Knowledge

A critical component of how successfully you are able to negotiate a settlement of your case will be how well you understand the law. There are many sources of information you can turn to for the basics of the law that will apply to your situation. You can start with the information available on:

- the Weinberger Divorce & Family Law Group website (located at www.WeinbergerLawGroup.com),
- the New Jersey Court System's Self-Help Resource Center website, found at the official New Jersey Courts website: http://bit.ly/njcourts, and
- Legal Services of New Jersey, which offers a downloadable divorce self-help guide (PDF) via their official site: http://bit.ly/lsnjlaw.

If there is some aspect of your case that is complex and that remains unclear to you after you have resorted to self-help, it will probably be well worth your while to obtain a consultation with an attorney prior to proceeding too far into negotiations with your spouse.

- - - -

FAQ: What Is Divorce Mediation?

Mediating your divorce is a popular out-of-court method for obtaining an uncontested divorce. When you mediate, you meet with a neutral third party (the mediator) whose role it is to guide you through the legal process of settling your issues and facilitate negotiations. A mediator is not a judge and does not make any rulings; the outcome of your divorce terms will still be entirely up to you and your spouse. During mediation, you may want to have an attorney help you. Private mediation is voluntary and non-binding. We offer a number of **mediation resources** on the Weinberger Mediation Center website, which is located at: http://bit.ly/mediation-center, to help you better understand this alternative.

FAQ: What Is Collaborative Divorce?
Some couples may be interested in pursuing a collaborative divorce, which like mediation, is another way to come together to reach an out-of-court, uncontested divorce settlement. Collaborative divorce requires each party to use an attorney and call in outside experts, if needed, to help parties reach agreements concerning certain issues, including child custody agreements. We have a more complete description of **collaborative divorce** on the Weinberger Divorce & Family Law Group website, which is located at: http://bit.ly/collaborative-divorce. If you wish to pursue this settlement method, be aware that collaborative divorce rules also require parties to hire new attorneys if the divorce cannot be resolved and ends up in court as a contested divorce. This is an incentive to help parties stay committed to working through negotiations.

- - - -

Practical Tip: Write Down All Questions.
As you read about the uncontested divorce process, keep a notebook handy to jot down all questions and concerns that come to mind. You can also print this book and place it in a binder to make it easier to underline and take notes right in the margin.

Step Four: When to Consult with an Attorney

Do you need a lawyer in order to get an uncontested divorce? This step requires you to do some deep thinking about whether or not you are likely to need attorney assistance in your case, and how you might go about finding the right attorney if you do.

For most people just starting out in the divorce process, a consultation with an attorney sooner rather than later can prevent costly mistakes. If you are hoping to proceed with your divorce as an uncontested matter and you are fairly certain that your spouse will be on board, you do not necessarily need to jump into hiring an attorney to provide you with full representation. If you are short of funds and your case is very simple, you may decide to represent yourself. Complete self-representation is a risky move in most cases, but it may be a reasonable decision to hire an attorney only for purposes of consultation during mediation, or only to prepare and/or review your Marital Settlement Agreement.

Many attorneys provide a free half hour or hour consultation and taking advantage of these offers early in your case can help you determine whether or not you are on the right track and can also help you decide exactly how much help you are likely to need and who you might want to hire. You do not have to decide about hiring an attorney immediately following a consultation, and you probably want to steer clear of anyone who employs high-pressure tactics to convince you to do so. Before consulting with an attorney, take some time first to read this entire book, organize your documents, clarify your goals for the outcome of your case, and educate yourself on New Jersey divorce law. This will help you decide how much attorney assistance you are likely to need. You then may want to consult with two or three attorneys to get some different perspectives about the track you are on.

What to Look for When Consulting with an Attorney

When you do have a consultation with an attorney, you will want to explain the extent to which you and your spouse agree as well as any areas you are still having trouble working out. An attorney will be able to tell you if the terms you are thinking about are workable and whether or not you will be giving up any important rights by going ahead with those terms. Be sure to ask about all possible outcomes in your case. If an attorney tries to discourage you from going through with the settlement terms you are considering, make sure that you understand the reasons for this recommendation. Even if you are largely in agreement with your soon-to-be-ex spouse, you may have some difficult decisions yet to make. Any attorney you ultimately hire should have the ability to help you make the best choices possible under all of the circumstances of your unique case.

The following are some of the things you may want to focus on when consulting with an attorney:

Family Law Experience

Regardless of whether you are planning on contesting any issues in your divorce, an attorney with substantial family law experience in the state will be able to determine whether or not you and your spouse are good candidates for uncontested divorce and whether any terms you are considering will ensure that your rights are protected in the divorce. The best way to ensure the right kind of experience is to choose an attorney or firm with a practice exclusively or primarily devoted to family law. If the attorney is certified by the New Jersey Supreme Court as a Matrimonial Law Attorney, or at least practices with a partner who has this kind of certification, that is an extra degree of insurance that the attorney or firm has superior knowledge and experience across a broad range of issues arising in family law practice.

Approach to Litigation

If you are committed to an uncontested route, you will want to rule out any attorney who is not settlement oriented and invested in looking for ways to help you amicably and civilly work out any remaining differences in your case. On the other hand, keep in mind that even a largely uncontested matter sometimes ends up requiring court intervention on one or two isolated aspects. Unless you are consulting with an attorney solely to finalize your MSA, you will also want to be sure that you have an attorney who will be assertive in protecting your interests if that proves necessary. Does the attorney have enough confidence not to back down in a critical situation and enough experience to know when going to court is the best available option? Being committed to the idea of an uncontested divorce should not mean walking away from your needs and rights. If an unexpected glitch appears in your case, would this attorney be competent in court, or would you have to hire a new attorney?

Costs

Find out what the attorney's hourly fee is and what kind of retainer the attorney will require to handle your case. Keep in mind that a retainer is just a deposit and rarely has much impact on the ultimate cost of a case. Try to get as good an estimate as possible of what your overall costs will be, bearing in mind that the cost of any legal matter can be difficult to predict at the outset of a case.

Ask the attorney if you are likely to need any expert opinions, including child psychologists and business valuation specialists, and whether sharing experts with your soon-to-be-ex would be an option.

If you decide to sign a retainer agreement, be sure to read it carefully. In addition to your attorney's hourly fee, in most cases, you will have to pay for copying costs, court filing costs, telephone and fax charges, delivery fees, and other miscellaneous costs. Legal cases are very paper-intensive. Copy fees alone can add up quickly. Ask the attorney what the typical filing fees and delivery fees are likely to be for each phase of your case.

Even if you think you have already worked out the terms of your settlement with your soon to be ex, be cautious about hiring any attorney who charges a flat fee. This type of arrangement can encourage an attorney to treat your situation as a simple cookie cutter matter, without stopping to consider whether an aspect is unique and requires special treatment—and if your case truly is almost finished without need for attorney assistance, the standard flat fee may well be too high. It is particularly important to be wary of services that provide pre-packaged do-it-yourself divorces. These are exactly what they say they are: You are doing it yourself, without legal advice. While this can certainly save you money up front, the long terms consequences of finalizing a divorce without legal advice can be disastrous.

Analysis of your Case

Make sure the attorney outlines the drawbacks of your situation as well as the upside. This is especially important if there are still aspects of your case about which you and your spouse are not in complete agreement. Be clear about what might happen if you fail to reach an agreement and be clear about whether or not any agreements you have already reached are legal and fair. While it may not be pleasant to hear that there is a chance that your uncontested matter could end up in court, it is better to realize this up front than to be surprised by it down the road.

Questions to Ask an Attorney During an Initial Consultation

Skills and Experience:
- How long have you been practicing family law?
- What percentage of your practice is family law?
- Are you certified in matrimonial law or is the head of the firm certified?
- Do you have any other specialized education or training in family law?
- If so, what is the specific nature of the education or training?
- How many family law trials have you handled?
- How many other family law court procedures have you handled?

Basic Strategy:
- Do you generally recommend mediation?
- Can you give me an overview of the mediation process?
- Do you recommend collaborative law?
- What percentage of your caseload goes to trial?
- How many of your cases settle through mediation?
- Under what circumstances might you feel that filing a motion in court or taking a case through the trial stage is the best option?

Specialized Knowledge:
- Do you have more experience in one area of family law (e.g., child custody, child support, property distribution, alimony) than in others?

- Are you personally familiar with experts (e.g., accountants, child psychologists, appraisers, private investigators) that may be relevant in any particular aspect of my case?

Case Management:
- How many attorneys are in your firm?
- Will you personally handle my case?
- How will we communicate: via phone, email, office appointments?
- Who will provide back-up if you are unavailable?
- Who will I be communicating with on a regular basis?
- How often do you accept or return phone calls?
- Do you prefer to communicate primarily by phone or primarily by email?

Costs:
- Will you require a retainer before starting work on my case?
- How much is the retainer?
- What is your hourly fee?
- What is the hourly fee of others in your firm who may be working on my case?
- What fees might I expect to incur as a result of hiring other professionals (e.g., accountants, child psychologists, appraisers, private investigators)?
- What other costs will I be responsible for beyond hourly fees?
- What are some of the different scenarios and contingencies that may affect the ultimate cost of my divorce?

> For an uncontested divorce, rule out any attorney who is not settlement-oriented and invested in ways to civilly resolve any differences.

Bari Z. Weinberger, Esq.

FAQ: Can Both of Us Use One Attorney?
It would be a conflict of interest for the same attorney to represent both spouses. Even spouses who are in complete agreement about settling their case have different legal interests and stand to lose or gain different rights or benefits. Sometimes a couple will reach agreement on terms, and then one spouse will hire an attorney to prepare the paperwork. In this situation, both spouses must understand that the attorney represents only the spouse who has hired the attorney. The other spouse is therefore at a potentially significant legal disadvantage and would be wise to have an independent attorney at least review the settlement agreement before finalizing terms.

- - - -

Practical Tip: Consult with An Attorney Even If You Decide to Use Divorce Mediation.
The best divorce mediators are often family law attorneys, but this does not mean that the mediator will protect your legal interests or act as an attorney for either spouse. As the mediator should explain to you at the beginning of the mediation process, only an attorney acting in a representative capacity can provide legal advice to an individual client. A family law mediator will provide legal information to both of you in a neutral manner but will not advocate for either of you.

Chapter 2

Tips to Keep in Mind When Engaging in Divorce Settlement Negotiations in New Jersey

Whether you end up negotiating face-to-face over the kitchen table or in a conference room with the assistance of a mediator, there are some practical tips to keep in mind that will help you to resolve your divorce case more efficiently and with a minimum of conflict:

Take Charge of Your Own Case

Even if you have hired an attorney to represent you in your uncontested divorce, remember that you are still in charge of making decisions in your case. Provide your attorney with complete and accurate facts, let the attorney explain how the law will apply to those facts, and then make reasonable decisions based on the facts and the law. Friends and relatives often have strong opinions that do not match either your own common-sense conclusions or your attorney's advice. Remember that emotion does not control what happens in a court case. Just because someone believes a certain result is "right" does not necessarily mean that result is probable or even possible from a legal standpoint. Ask your attorney as many questions as you need to and listen carefully to the answers. Make sure you understand both the best case and the worst-case scenario. If necessary, ask for clarification about what aspects of your case will be controlled by fact and law and what aspects would be left largely up to the discretion of a judge. Be sure to be clear with your attorney as to your expectations so that the attorney can advise you on the strengths or weaknesses of those expectations from a legal perspective.

Begin Settlement Efforts Early

No matter what stage your case has reached, settling as early as possible will almost always save you money and help you avoid further emotional stress. If you and your spouse can sit down together and hash out your differences without attorneys, this is all for the best. While you will generally benefit from hiring attorneys to draft or review your settlement agreement, the more you can agree on first, the better.

Cultivate a Spirit of Cooperation

If you and your spouse have already hired attorneys and retreated to strongly opposed positions, do not be afraid to be the first to extend an olive branch. Provided that you are able to remain calm and collected when negotiating with your spouse, this is likely to be a worthwhile endeavor. If you feel too much anger or guilt to be able to keep a clear head, get some help with addressing these emotions. A good therapist can often be a valuable ally and may be able to work with you on relaxation and stress relief techniques while also helping to keep you on track in your settlement efforts.

Use Negotiation Tactics Wisely

There are many approaches to negotiation and people tend to develop their own styles and their own sets of tactics. Some people begin with extremely high demands, believing that it will then seem as though they have sacrificed a lot just by becoming more reasonable. Other people start close to their bottom line and immediately declare that they will not budge an inch. In general, it is probably best to start off by asking for everything that you want, since if you do not ask for something, there is little chance that you will get it. The most important thing, however, is to have an understanding for yourself of exactly where you are and are not willing to compromise. Try to avoid having only one fallback position. Think about different ways that a deal could be structured and balanced. Have a strategy in mind and be flexible whenever possible.

> Know your true bottom line; know when to get help… and know how much help you need.

Bari Z. Weinberger, Esq.

The Art of Compromise: Steps to Successful Divorce Negotiations

Even in the best of settlements, each party must generally give something up. Think about what each of you is asking for and consider whether or not one of you has already given up more than the other. People usually have a lot of difficulty evaluating their own situations in an objective manner. Try to put yourself in your spouse's shoes and see things from that perspective. Consider what would make things easier for your spouse and decide if there is something you can offer with which you are willing to make a compromise.

When assessing the adequacy of your agreement, look at the entire package rather than focusing narrowly on a single issue. The more important any one goal is to you, the more you may have to compromise to achieve it. Be very careful in making any one goal all-important, as you may end up with an overall result that will not work well for you in the long run. For example, many people have an emotional attachment to the family home and negotiate very hard to keep it, only to find that they have not come away with enough income to maintain the home or have given up all their retirement assets at an age when such assets will be impossible to recoup.

When negotiations work, both parties can walk away feeling satisfied and agreeable with the outcome of their divorce. To boost your chances for successfully negotiating your divorce, consider these time-tested negotiation techniques:

Find Out What Your Spouse Wants

Before making your desired outcomes for the divorce known, take the time to listen to your spouse and find out what he or she really wants. This tactic helps with negotiating for two reasons. First, when people feel listened to and have the sense that their views are being taken seriously, it goes a long way to lowering the tension in the room; listening to your spouse's needs means your spouse will probably be more willing to listen to your own. Secondly, understanding what your spouse wants can help you identify some possible bargaining chips. If she wants the vacation home, but you want a greater percentage of the stock portfolio and secretly don't care about having a second home, having this kind of information can be an easy way to quickly negotiate an outcome you both find acceptable.

Prioritize What You Want

It might be nice to keep the living room furniture set you worked overtime to afford. But if comes down to digging in about the furniture versus paying your spouse a little less in monthly alimony because she gets her wish to keep most of the contents of the house — which one sounds better? As you establish a bottom line, think about what's best for your future finances, your family's future, and what you are willing to give up in order to get a better life moving forward.

Get the Momentum Going

You may have a feeling (or know outright) that a fight over child custody or alimony is looming. To set the stage for more peaceful discussions about these kinds of hot button issues, try to reach agreement on as many smaller issues as you can to get momentum going in your negotiations. Discussing hard to solve issues first tends to derail negotiations because it can lead to tension that spills over onto the issues that follow. After battling through child custody negotiations, for example, suddenly that flat screen TV that you were willing to let go of may seem like a huge deal, and another fight erupts. Your divorce attorney can help you identify issues in your divorce that should be easy to settle.

State Your Position, Not Your Demands

Before sitting down to negotiate, take time to formulate your position on the issues, being careful to use language that states a position rather than putting forth a demand. A position reflects a legitimate, broad interest rather than consisting of a black and white demand. For example, stating that you need to spend significant time with your children in your home because you believe that children need two involved and effective parents is a fair position; stating that you **must** have the children stay overnight in your home every Monday, Tuesday and Thursday is a black and white demand.

Whenever you and your spouse are having trouble reaching an agreement, try to identify the true interest at the bottom of each demand. This will often open the door to alternate possibilities and can go a long way toward maximizing positive results for everyone. For example, instead of telling your spouse, "I want our child 50 percent of the time," try something along the lines of, "Our child loves both of us. And we both love him. As such, I think 50/50 parenting time gives our child the best option to continue developing loving relationships with both of us." If needed, write these position statements out beforehand and have them in front of you during negotiations.

Create Win-Win Scenarios

In drafting your position statements, also consider ways you can frame settlement options as something that solves a problem for both of you. In negotiations over the family home, for example, instead of telling your spouse, "I want the house," try explaining the situation in more win-win terms: "Our house is old and requires frequent repairs. I made most of the repairs while we lived there and did so inexpensively compared to hiring a repairman. If you want the house you will end up spending a lot of money for repairs, including the new roof we both know is needed. Also, I will need to find another place to live, costing us both more money in the end. So, to reduce costs for both of us, I think it's better if I live in the home and you receive your equity share."

Check Your Ego (And Emotions) At the Door

The end of a marriage is almost never without emotional fallout. However, know that bringing anger, frustration, and jealously into the negotiating room — and making decisions based on purely emotional reasons — is an almost surefire way to not get what you want in the long run (for more on this, please read Bari Weinberger's Huffington Post article, Divorce: Take Time for Emotional Clarity in Decisions, located at http://bit.ly/emotional-clarity). Whether it takes seeing a therapist, buying a punching bag, meditating, or just watching funny movie and having a laugh with a friend, do everything you can to be in a more neutral frame of mind when you sit down at the negotiating table.

Know When to Get Help

There are some situations where face-to-face negotiation between spouses is unworkable. If you and your spouse have a volatile relationship, negotiating without a third-party present may prove difficult, or even unwise. In this type of situation, moving on to mediation, or even to attorney-assisted negotiation, in which your attorneys do the talking for you, may be necessary. Mediation provides the opportunity to organize your paperwork and sit down with a neutral party who has experience in working with couples in your situation. You can find more information about family law mediation on our Weinberger Mediation Center website, located at: http://bit.ly/mediation-center. If you and your spouse are having trouble seeing eye-to-eye on only a few items, one or two mediation sessions may be enough to get you both on the same track. An experienced mediator may also be able to help you develop ideas you have not thought of that will maximize positive outcomes for both of you. If you feel that your spouse is in a more powerful position than you are or if for any reason you are intimidated by your spouse, consult an attorney prior to mediation and make sure that you know where you will and will not take a hard stance. It is much easier to negotiate if you know your bottom line.

Know How Much Help You Need

If you and your spouse cannot agree in mediation, or if you feel that you are being taken advantage of, it may be time to have your attorneys talk to each other. If you and your spouse can agree on certain parts of your settlement but not on others, incorporate these agreements that you have into a written document to be reviewed by your counsel.

Chapter 3

Marital Settlement Agreements

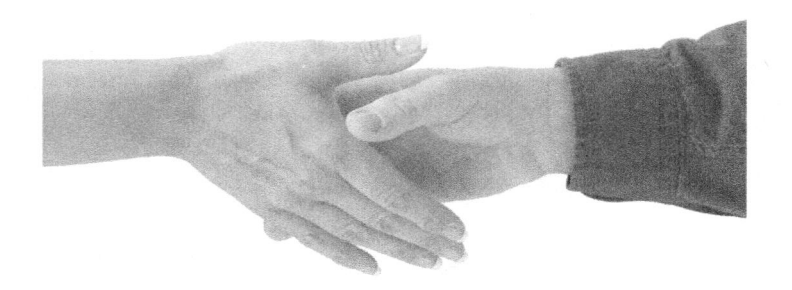

If you and your spouse succeed in settling all of your issues, you can enter into a Marital Settlement Agreement (MSA). MSA's are also sometimes called "Property Settlement Agreements."

The MSA is a legal document spelling out the terms of your divorce and establishing a framework for your relationship with each other going forward as former spouses.

New Jersey couples who are able to work out their differences can choose an uncontested divorce process at the outset of their divorce case. Couples who start out in a contested process always have the option of negotiating an MSA and converting to an uncontested divorce during the case.

Depending on your individual situation, your MSA should address some or all of the following:

- Distribution of assets (including real property, personal property, vehicles, bank accounts and retirement accounts or plans, etc.)
- Division of debts
- Child custody and parenting time
- Child support, including expenses such as medical bills, tuition, day care costs, camp fees, activity fees, and education expenses
- Alimony
- Health and/or life insurance obligations
- Tax considerations, and
- Any other important and legally enforceable issue related to the divorce.

You will need to include the terms of any agreements with your former spouse that you want a court to be able to enforce in your written MSA and make the terms as specific as possible. Your agreement should also include a plan for negotiating any future disagreements. For example, you may want to agree that you will attend mediation before either of you files any court papers relating to the terms of your MSA.

> By formalizing your Marital Settlement Agreement in court and making it part of your divorce decree, you will be waiving your right to a trial.

Bari Z. Weinberger, Esq.

Legal Effects of the Marital Settlement Agreement

Once you and your spouse have signed your MSA, you will both be bound by the terms. The MSA is generally also incorporated into the final decree of divorce so that it becomes enforceable as a court order. All or part of the agreement may also be merged with the divorce decree, which can affect its enforceability as a contract. Your attorney can give you more information about how and under what circumstances a court is likely to enforce your MSA.

Consult with an Attorney Before Finalizing a Marital Settlement Agreement

Even if you and your spouse have developed a basic agreement addressing all of your issues, you should each consult with individual attorneys before finalizing an MSA. An attorney can review your draft MSA or prepare a comprehensive MSA from start to finish. It is important to understand that by formalizing your MSA in court and making it part of your divorce decree, you will be waiving your right to a trial. For this reason, you need to have some idea of how the MSA you are considering would compare with the results you might obtain in court. An attorney can advise you about this and can also advise you further about the benefits you may be gaining by settling your case early, including the time and cost savings. An attorney can also make sure that your MSA is valid and will hold up in court.

Amending Your Marital Settlement Agreement

You and your spouse can amend your MSA in the future if you both agree to do so. If you have a disagreement about enforcing or interpreting the MSA after your divorce has been finalized, you can negotiate a solution or file a motion in court. Even if you and your spouse enter into an MSA, the court keeps the power to modify terms relating to child custody and support in the event of a substantial change in circumstances. Terms relating to alimony are also modifiable unless your MSA specifically states that they are not. Terms relating to asset and debt distribution cannot usually be changed once the divorce is final.

What to Do If Settlement Efforts Fail

If you find yourselves stuck in negotiations on one or more issues and unable to proceed with an uncontested divorce, you will have additional chances to settle your case during the contested court process. The New Jersey Supreme Court has established procedures to ensure that parties to a contested divorce have several opportunities to engage in complementary (also known as "alternative") dispute resolution processes, such as mediation and arbitration, prior to trial. Parties can also choose to attend private mediation at any time during an ongoing case.

In some cases it truly will not be possible to come to a reasonable settlement. While the first option to consider when negotiations stall will usually be mediation, if one spouse refuses to give an inch and is demanding clearly inappropriate results, mediation may also be unsuccessful. In some situations, mediation is not a viable alternative. If there is any history of domestic violence between spouses, then mediation is generally not advisable. It will also sometimes not be a realistic alternative if one spouse has an intimidating style, or if one spouse is simply very meek or unwilling to ask for anything. A good mediator can sometimes help couples succeed even in these types of situations, but there are no guarantees.

If negotiation and mediation efforts have not been successful in your case, before assuming that litigation is inevitable, consider the possibility of arbitration. Private arbitration is similar to a trial but generally simpler and faster. Couples can submit a single issue or several issues to an arbitrator, but be aware that an arbitrator's ruling is binding, meaning that by taking part in the arbitration process, you agree to what the arbitrator decides.

Settling all of your issues successfully means paving the way for an uncontested divorce. Good settlement negotiations during a contested case can even result in changing a contested divorce into an uncontested one.

You can find more information on both mediation and arbitration on the Weinberger Mediation Center website located at: http://bit.ly/mediation-center.

Chapter 4

Step-By-Step Procedural Requirements for An Uncontested Divorce

The New Jersey uncontested divorce process provides an efficient means of obtaining a judgment of divorce. Still, divorcing couples who choose this route must understand that the process requires completion of a specific series of procedural steps. Following these steps in the correct order is critical to ensuring that the court will expeditiously grant your divorce.

Preparing a Complaint

All married couples will legally begin an action for divorce in New Jersey with a Complaint for Divorce.* If you and your spouse agree to proceed with an uncontested divorce, you can resolve all your issues and prepare your MSA before either of you files a complaint. If one of you has already filed a complaint, you can still proceed through an uncontested process by negotiating a prompt settlement of all of your issues.

- - - -

* If you are ending a domestic partnership or a civil union, the procedural steps you will follow are virtually the same as those you would follow in pursuing a divorce. Domestic partnership terminations tend to involve fewer legal issues than either divorces or dissolutions of civil unions, but the procedures are still essentially the same. If you entered into a legal marriage, civil union, or domestic partnership in another state or country and then moved to New Jersey, you will be able to formally terminate your relationship in New Jersey once you have satisfied the residency requirements.

- - - -

Deciding Who is the Plaintiff and Who is the Defendant

The spouse who files the complaint is the "plaintiff" and the other spouse is the "defendant." While there is sometimes a slight tactical advantage in being the plaintiff in a contested matter, there is rarely any benefit in an uncontested matter. Although one spouse always files the complaint, if both spouses agree ahead of time on all or most of the details, the defendant spouse may file an answer that contains essentially the same information as the complaint or may choose not to file an answer at all, allowing the court to enter a default judgment based only on the information in the complaint. You can find more information on uncontested divorce by default judgment in the next chapter.

Residency Requirements

For a New Jersey court to have jurisdiction over a divorce, at least one of the spouses must be a resident of the county in which the case is filed, and in most cases, one spouse must have been a resident of the state for a full one-year period immediately preceding initiation of the case.

Special Residency Requirements for Servicemembers

In general, a servicemember or spouse of a servicemember may choose to file a complaint for divorce in the state where the spouse resides, in the state where the servicemember is stationed, or in the state where the servicemember claims legal residence. The latter can be either the servicemember's home state or the state where the servicemember plans to live after leaving the service. The home state or "home of record" will be designated in the servicemember's periodic payment record, known as the Leave and Earnings Statement (LES).

If you are in the service or married to someone in the service, you should think carefully about when and where to initiate a divorce case. While filing a complaint where the servicemember is currently stationed may be convenient in the short-term, it will be much less convenient if that state retains jurisdiction after both of you have moved to different states. While this tends to be less of a concern in uncontested divorces, if your case involves alimony payments or any child-related issues, it is always possible that one of you may want to return to court at some future date even after the divorce is final. A court will normally grant a motion to transfer jurisdiction if neither party remains in the state, but if spouses or former spouses reside in different states and each wants the matter transferred to a different court, the motion could be conflict-ridden, time-consuming, and expensive.

If the two of you have children together, you will also need to consider the children's residency. Pursuant to the Uniform Child Custody Jurisdiction and Enforcement Act (UCCJEA), a state court will not ordinarily have jurisdiction over matters of child custody unless the children have physically resided in that state for at least the past six months. So, for example, if you have been living in Virginia with your children for the past six months and you decide to file for divorce in New Jersey where your military spouse is stationed, the New Jersey family court would not be able to enter orders controlling the custody and visitation of your children.

Information to Include in the Complaint

If you are the plaintiff, you will generally have to provide the following information:

- name and current address for both you and your spouse,*
- the date and place of your marriage,
- the grounds for divorce, and any necessary supporting information (such as timing of marriage breakdown, or separation date),
- confirmation that the residency requirement has been satisfied,
- any additional addresses you used during the time the grounds for divorce arose,
- names and ages of any children,
- list of any prior legal actions between you and your spouse, and
- description of the relief you are requesting in the case.

- - - -

*Victims of domestic violence have the option of providing a post office box number or substitute address and phone number.

Grounds

The complaint must state a reason for the divorce, known as "grounds." If you and your spouse have agreed to pursue an uncontested divorce, or if you are simply hoping to proceed with as little conflict as possible, choosing a no-fault ground will start you off on the path to an uncontested process.

Grounds available for divorce in New Jersey without any allegation of fault include:

- **Irreconcilable Differences.** This refers to a breakdown of the marriage lasting 6 months or longer, without a reasonable prospect of reconciliation. The parties are not required to provide any information about the circumstances leading to the breakdown.

- **Separation.** Couples who have lived apart (meaning lived in separate residences) for at least 18 months can file for divorce on the basis of separation. No other circumstances are necessary.

The New Jersey law describing grounds for divorce is N.J.S.A 2A:34-2. For more information on grounds for divorce in New Jersey, see the Weinberger Divorce & Family Law Group website: http://bit.ly/divorcegrounds.

> You must state a reason, known as grounds…choosing a no-fault ground will start you on the uncontested divorce process.

Bari Z. Weinberger, Esq.

Request for Relief

Although the specifics of whatever relief you are requesting, such as dollar amounts for support or detailed schedules for parenting time, can be left to work out later, it is important to include in your complaint a general request for any relief you believe you may need at any point during the development of your case. If you already have a signed MSA, you can indicate the relief you and your spouse have included in the MSA. A New Jersey divorce complaint can include a request for some or all of the following relief (and more):

- alimony (also known as spousal support or spousal maintenance),
- equitable property distribution, including division of real and personal property and allocation of debts,
- custody of minor children,
- parenting time with minor children,
- child support, and
- restoration of former name.

Filing Documents with the Court

New Jersey Court Rules require a plaintiff in a divorce case to file the complaint in the county where the cause of action (grounds for divorce) arose. This may be the county where either spouse currently resides, or, depending on the facts included in the complaint, may be a county of previous residence. If you are uncertain where to file your case, an attorney can advise you. After determining where to file, you, or your attorney, should send the court the original and two copies of your complaint and all supporting documents, and keep two additional copies of everything filed for your own use.

Depending on the circumstances of your particular case, you will need to file all or most of the following with your complaint:

- **Certification of Verification and Non-Collusion.** This is a sworn statement attached to the complaint verifying that all of the claims and facts included are true; that there are no other actions currently pending in a court or arbitration venue involving you and your spouse (or identifying any actions that are pending); and that there are no other people who should be named in the current case.

- **Certification of Insurance.** This is a form attached to the complaint listing all known insurance coverage for you, your spouse, and your minor children, including health, life, homeowners or renters, automobile, or any other type of insurance. Coverage in effect at the date of filing cannot be cancelled during the case without court approval or consent of the parties.

- **Certification of Notification of Complementary Dispute Resolution Alternatives.** This is a form attached to the complaint which states that you have received information from the court or your attorney explaining the availability of dispute resolution alternatives such as mediation and arbitration. If you are represented by an attorney, the attorney must provide you with this information and will also sign the certification.

- **Family Part Case Information Statement (CIS).** A CIS is a financial disclosure statement requiring detailed financial information and copies of certain documents such as tax returns and pay stubs.

- The CIS is found at the New Jersey Courts official website: http://bit.ly/nj-cis. Both spouses are required to file a CIS within 20 days of a defendant's answer or appearance in any New Jersey case in which there are contested issues regarding children, property division, or spousal support. Even if you have settled all of your issues, it is always a good idea for both spouses to file a CIS, as this helps ensure full disclosure of all financial information on both sides and will bolster the enforceability of any MSA the spouses enter into. You must update your CIS any time there is a change in financial circumstances, and you must keep a copy of it until the conclusion of all financial matters in your case, including completion of any required alimony payments.

- **Confidential Litigant Information Sheet (CLIS).** You must include this form if you are requesting alimony or child support. It contains detailed personal information, including date and place of birth, social security number, driver's license number, license plate number, mother's maiden name, children's social security numbers, and medical information. It is not attached to the complaint and is kept out of the public record as a confidential document. The purpose of the form is to provide information that will enable the court to contact you when necessary to establish, modify, or enforce orders in your case. The CLIS is available at the New Jersey Courts official website: http://bit.ly/nj-clis.

- **Request for Waiver of Fees and Supporting Certification and Order Waiving Fees.** If you are unable to afford the court filing fees you may be eligible for a fee waiver. You must submit appropriate forms with a waiver request. A Filing Fee Waiver Request Packet is available from the New Jersey Courts official website: http://bit.ly/request-packet.

- **Filing Fees and Self-Addressed Stamped Envelope.** To complete the filing and return date-stamped copies of the filed documents, the court will require a cover letter requesting such copies, payment of any applicable filing fees, and a self-addressed, stamped envelope large enough to hold the copies being returned.

Serving the Complaint

After you file your complaint, you must serve it, along with a summons and proof of service form, on your spouse. There are several ways to accomplish this, including personal service, service by mail, substituted service on a special agent, or service by publication. In an uncontested divorce, you will probably know that your spouse is willing to accept service, and you can therefore use the simplest and least expensive method, which is usually service by regular and certified mail, with return receipt requested. Your spouse should return a signed and notarized "acknowledgment of service" form to you. You will then file the acknowledgment with the court. If your spouse is represented by an attorney, the attorney can generally also accept service on your spouse's behalf.

Service of Process on a Servicemember

A spouse can serve a member of the military who is off-post in the same manner as a civilian, as state law will govern such a situation. Service on-post can be more complicated as many military bases are closed to civilian access, and some military properties are on land with shared or even exclusive federal jurisdiction. In most cases there will be a centralized procedure for service. If you and your spouse agree about proceeding with an uncontested divorce, service should not be a major issue. Nevertheless, you should both be aware that even if the servicemember accepts service voluntarily, you may face delays in your case in the event of deployment. If you know that your spouse will be deployed overseas in the near future and you have an urgent matter such as child support that you would like to have a court order for (even if you agree about the support amount), your best approach will usually be to complete service before the deployment if at all possible. Military families can visit the official American Bar Association "Home Front" website at: http://bit.ly/abahomefront to obtain additional information about applicable laws, including a more in-depth explanation of the SCRA.

Responding to a Complaint

A defendant has 35 days from the date of service to respond to the complaint. The parties can agree to an extension of up to 60 days before the expiration of the initial 35-day period. The court can also grant a longer extension on request. A defendant can respond by doing any of the following:

Entering an Appearance

A defendant, or an attorney for the defendant, can enter an appearance in the case by returning the notarized acknowledgement of service to the plaintiff or by filing a general appearance with the court. A defendant who enters an appearance without filing an answer retains the option to contest some or all of the relief requested in the complaint at a later stage of the case.

Filing an Answer

A defendant can also enter an appearance in the case by filing an answer admitting or denying each allegation in the complaint.

Filing an Answer with a Counterclaim

Along with an answer, defendant can file a counterclaim, which is very similar to an original complaint, to assert the same or different grounds for divorce, or to seek affirmative relief from the court such as custody, alimony and/or child support. If you are served with a complaint for divorce and you have an unresolved claim for custody, alimony and or child support from your spouse, see the information pages on Contested Divorce on the Weinberger Divorce & Family Law Group website: http://bit.ly/contested-divorce for further explanation, or contact an attorney to find out if filing a counterclaim is necessary in your case.

Chapter 5

Default Judgments in Uncontested Divorce

If the defendant fails to answer the complaint within 35 days of service, the spouse filing the complaint may pursue a default judgment. Spouses who have agreed to terms of settlement between themselves can complete an uncontested divorce by default judgment by following the procedures outlined here.

Although the defendant will not answer the complaint, the parties will need to have a signed marital settlement agreement (MSA) before the default hearing to ensure protection of both parties' interests. While a CIS is not required in this kind of uncontested situation, it is a good policy for the plaintiff to prepare one to ensure full financial disclosure.

Request for Default
After 35 days have passed since the date of service, the plaintiff, or the plaintiff's attorney, files a request for default judgment with the court, asking the court to enter a judgment of divorce without a trial due to defendant's failure to answer the complaint. In order to avoid additional paperwork and costs, a plaintiff must make this request within 6 months of the expiration of defendant's time to respond.

Affidavit of Non-Military Service
Because active servicemembers may experience extended absences from the country and consequently have difficulty responding to court documents in a timely manner, the Servicemembers Civil Relief Act (SCRA) protects them from default judgments. For this reason, a plaintiff requesting default must file a document verifying that the defendant is not a member of the military. If either you or your spouse is in the military, the military spouse can waive the protection of the SCRA to allow the default to go forward. Consult an attorney with experience in military divorce to be sure that the waiver is in the correct form.

*The **Certification of Non-Military Service** form is available from the official New Jersey Courts website: http://bit.ly/non-military.*

Default Hearing

The court will set a date for a default hearing. The plaintiff should send the defendant a notice of the default hearing by regular and certified mail, return receipt requested. The plaintiff, or the plaintiff's attorney, should also prepare a proposed judgment of divorce, attach the MSA to the proposed judgment, and serve these papers on the defendant at least 20 days prior to the hearing. Although only the plaintiff is required to attend the hearing, the best approach is for both spouses to attend. The hearing will then proceed as an uncontested divorce hearing, and the judge will usually enter a judgment incorporating the MSA into the judgment of divorce. You can find an explanation of the types of questions that an attorney or a judge will ask at an uncontested divorce hearing later in this book.

> "After 35 days have passed since the date of service, the plaintiff can file a request with the court to enter a judgment of divorce without a trial."

Bari Z. Weinberger, Esq.

Uncontested Divorce by Default

In many counties in New Jersey there are procedures available permitting the parties to proceed by default and file their MSA with the court without attending a hearing. This can be a simple and cost-effective method of obtaining a divorce, as it saves the defendant the expense of filing an answer and saves both parties the time and inconvenience involved in participating in a hearing.

If you and your spouse would like to take advantage of this option, you must consult the county where you are filing your case to make sure that you qualify for the procedure and that you comply with all applicable rules. The plaintiff will generally have to submit a certified statement including the information that the court would have taken testimony and evidence on in a hearing. Both parties will have to certify that they entered into the MSA knowingly and willingly; that the MSA resolves all issues in the case; that the parties consider the MSA to be fair and appropriate; that they waive rights to a trial; and that they are satisfied with the legal services provided to them. The plaintiff must also specifically request that the MSA be incorporated in the judgment of divorce.

Rules regarding uncontested divorce vary by county, and within each county, rules often change as local laws are updated. For the most accurate picture of what is required by your county/vicinage to complete an uncontested divorce, contact your local family law department and ask.

Family Law Departments

Street addresses and websites for the Family Law Departments can be found at the New Jersey Courts official website, located at: http://bit.ly/fl-addresses.

Chapter 6

Uncontested Divorce after Defendant Files an Answer or Appearance

If the defendant spouse files an answer or enters an appearance in the case, the case will be set down on the court calendar for a Case Management Conference (CMC) and assigned to a procedural track.

Case Management and Discovery In An Uncontested Case

New Jersey Court Rules provide that all civil family law cases, except for summary judgment matters, must follow one of four tracks: priority, complex, expedited, or standard. The New Jersey Court Rule governing Case Management Conferences (CMC's) in civil family cases is Rule 5:5-7. Section (a) discusses priority and complex actions, and section (b) discusses standard and expedited cases. All cases identified as uncontested prior to or at the CMC will be assigned to the expedited track.

Because the courts try to resolve uncontested cases and other relatively simple divorce cases in as timely a manner as possible, the court rules require an initial CMC in an expedited case to be held within 30 days after expiration of the deadline for filing the last responsive pleading (either defendant's answer or plaintiff's answer to defendant's counterclaim). If the court sets a discovery deadline at the CMC, the date must be no more than 90 days after service of the original complaint. If you and your spouse are attempting to settle your case but you have not reached agreement on every issue by the date of the CMC, you will have to update the court on your progress and consider whether any formal discovery is necessary in your case.

"Discovery" refers to court procedures for exchanging information in the case. One of the benefits of agreeing early to an uncontested divorce is the ability to bypass formal discovery, which can be expensive and time-consuming, and instead exchange information voluntarily, thus facilitating an out-of-court settlement. Often the only piece of discovery exchanged by parties to an uncontested case is the New Jersey Family Part Case Information Statement (CIS).

The Case Information Statement

The CIS is a document containing detailed financial information. Although it can be very time consuming to fill out, taking the time and care to complete an accurate CIS is essential in a contested case and highly recommended even in the simplest uncontested case. Parties must sign their CIS under penalty of perjury, must amend the CIS if there are any changes in the original information during the course of the case, and must be sure to file any amendments with the court no later than 20 days before a final hearing.

Your CIS provides the other party, the attorneys, and the judge with a snapshot of your income, assets and debts, the amount of money you need to live on each month, and any income available for support of minor children or the other spouse. If you are still negotiating settlement terms, the information in the CIS can provide the basis for calculation of any applicable child support as well as negotiation and structuring of alimony and equitable property distribution. You must include all of the following information in your CIS, which is broken into steps A-G as follows:

Part A: **Personal Information**

In Part A of the CIS, you will need to provide detailed information about you and your family, including birthdates, marriage and separation dates, and a list of the outstanding issues in your case.

" Your Case Information Statement provides a snapshot of income, assets, and debts and can be used to calculate alimony and child support. "

Bari Z. Weinberger, Esq.

Parts B & C: **Employment and Income**

In Parts B and C, you will need to provide information about your employer, your annual income for the past year, your spouse's annual income for the past year, and what you know to be your current year to date income. The information must be accurate and supported with paystubs, W-2s and tax returns, whenever possible. You must also provide information about pay frequency and additional sources of income beyond base pay, including such things as stock options, bonuses, commissions, and any non-employment related income.

Part D: **Monthly Expenses**

Part D of the CIS requires detailed information on monthly family expenses based on the marital standard of living, as well as current living expenses for couples who have already established separate residences. The former should reflect actual expenses of the marital lifestyle, and the latter should reflect actual current expenses for yourself and any children currently residing with you. While the amounts will necessarily include some estimates, it is important not to estimate too loosely and to provide exact figures whenever possible. If you are ever called upon to testify as to the figures you provide, you will have to have some proofs or basis for the numbers reflected in your budget. If you paid for most of your expenses with a credit card, debit card or by check, you should be able to compile estimates based on a review of your financial statements. Be sure to review statements for several months to obtain an average rather than relying on a single month, as expenses normally vary somewhat from month to month. Do not forget to include a monthly percentage for amounts paid annually or according to some other periodic schedule. To obtain a monthly figure for amounts paid weekly, multiply the amount by 4.3.

The purpose of the detailed budget is to help the parties and the court calculate whether or not the amount of available income is sufficient to meet each party's actual expenses. Sometimes when spouses physically separate and two households need to be maintained on the same amount of income that formerly supported one, they will have to liquidate and sell assets to make ends meet or tighten their respective belts. The CIS documents also help the parties and the court identify assets which may be available for sale and the probable proceeds that could be realized in this fashion.

After you have completed your budget, carefully evaluate whether or not the total amount makes sense in light of the money that you actually spent each month during your marriage or that you are actually spending now. If amounts seem to be missing, reconsider items you may have overlooked. Although the CIS form is broken down into categories to assist parties in identifying all usual and major expenses, it is still surprisingly easy to overlook minor expenses that may add up, or to underestimate the amount spent monthly on critical items such as groceries and household supplies.

Another common error is to estimate current expenses as an incorrect percentage of marital expenses. For example, expenses for three people living in the same house that four people formerly lived in would usually be significantly higher than three-fourths of the previous amount. Major expenses such as rent, and mortgage are generally stable regardless of the number of people benefitting from the expenditure. Be sure to estimate actual expenses whenever possible rather than relying on percentages that may not be accurate.

Part D of the CIS requires completion of three separate schedules, as follows:

- **Shelter.** This category includes rental or mortgage payments, as well as payments for electricity, gas, water, sewer, telephone, cable, internet, homeowner's or renter's insurance, property taxes, repairs and maintenance, garbage and snow removal, landscaping charges, and any other monthly costs related to renting or owning your home.

- **Transportation.** This category includes monthly lease or loan payments on a car or other vehicle used for transportation, insurance premiums on any such vehicle, gasoline expenses, costs of repairs and maintenance, license and registration fees, commuter train or bus fare, and other costs related to transportation.

- **Personal Expenses.** Personal expenses include all of your other costs such as groceries, health insurance premiums, and unreimbursed expenses for medical, dental, or vision care, prescription drugs, and therapy or psychological counseling. You should also include payments to domestic employees or professionals such as accountants. If you and your spouse contributed on a regular basis to cash savings or retirement accounts, include these amounts as well. Be careful not to overlook items such as gift and entertainment expenses (including but not limited to birthday gifts, holiday gifts, special occasions), vacation costs, and the costs of personal services such as hair care. Monthly personal expenses also include child related costs such as babysitting or day care costs, private school tuition, camp fees, club dues, and any costs associated with sports, hobbies, or lessons. Include any support obligations you may have from previous relationships in your personal expenses as well.

Part E: **Assets and Liabilities**

Part E of the CIS requires you to identify your marital and separate assets and liabilities. You must provide information regarding all existing checking and savings accounts, real estate holdings, timeshares, IRAs, pensions, Keoghs, ESOPs, SEPs, SSPs, 403b or 401k plans, mutual funds, stocks and bonds, and other investments. You will also need to include a detailed description of any leased or owned vehicle, including the year, make, model, value, and titled owner. Any business interests, collectibles, or other personal property with significant value should be itemized in Part E. If you or your spouse has a whole life insurance policy with cash value, list the current cash value as of the date you complete your CIS.

In the liabilities section of Part E, provide information regarding any real estate mortgages, lines of credit, long-term debts such as student loans, revolving charges such as credit cards, short-term debts for items such as financed purchases or medical bills, and any contingent liabilities. You must specify the total amount due and the due date as well as the monthly payment. If you owe money to family members, friends or business colleagues, make sure to include information about these debts as well, so that the obligation will be considered during the equitable distribution in the case.

Part F: **Special Issues**

In Part F, you should identify any special problems or challenges that you have not already addressed elsewhere in the CIS, if these are likely to have an impact on the case. For example, if you will need a forensic accountant to value a family business or you have a child with special needs, you should make a note of such circumstances in Schedule F.

Part G: **Attachments**

Part G provides a checklist of required attachments such as W-2 forms, pay stubs and tax returns. Review this to ensure that you have provided all necessary supporting documents.

Additional Discovery Tools

You can ordinarily bypass formal tools such as interrogatories, requests for production or admissions, or depositions if you are pursuing an uncontested divorce.

> *You can find more information about the discovery process on the Weinberger Divorce & Family Law Group website, located at: http://bit.ly/formal-discovery.*

Sometimes spouses who are proceeding through an uncontested process need to obtain expert opinions regarding the value of real estate, a pension, or a business or professional practice. A spouse may also require a vocational evaluation to determine appropriate future employment or earning capacity. Parents may want to consult with a child custody expert to affirm that a proposed parenting plan is on the right track. If both parties agree to these evaluations, they can acquire joint experts to prepare reports and divide the costs. This is a common course of action in mediation or collaborative law.

Chapter 7

The Uncontested Divorce Hearing

As soon as you and your spouse reach an agreement on all issues, you should inform the court of your settlement and request an uncontested hearing. If you are either the plaintiff or a defendant who filed a counterclaim, you may be required to attend the hearing. If you are the defendant but you have not filed a counterclaim, you are not generally required to go, but the best approach is for you to go as well.

While you may feel anxious that you still have to go to court, this hearing will be brief and straightforward. You can relax knowing that the hard work is done, and the hearing is just a formality. Your attorney (or the judge if you do not have an attorney) will ask you a series of questions. Your attorney will let you know in advance exactly what questions you will have to answer, and because the hearing is uncontested, you do not have to worry about being cross-examined by your spouse's attorney. The most important thing is to be sure that you bring all of your completed paperwork to court. You must also be absolutely sure that your CIS is up to date at least 20 days prior to the final hearing.

Questions to Expect at the Hearing

These are some examples of the types of questions you can expect to answer at an uncontested divorce hearing. The actual questions may differ somewhat, but in general, you can expect:

Background questions, such as:
- the date of your marriage,
- your place of residence,
- whether your birth date and social security number have been accurately entered into the court records,
- the names and birthdates of any joint children, and
- (if applicable), whether you wish to resume your pre-marital surname;

Questions establishing the cause of action for divorce:
- the grounds for the divorce (irreconcilable differences, separation, etc.), and
- whether there is any chance of reconciliation;

Questions about your legal representation, such as:
- whether you have been represented by an attorney throughout the proceedings,
- whether you are satisfied with the legal representation you have received, and
- whether all your legal questions have been answered;

Questions to verify that you understand the MSA, such as:
- whether you are under the influence of any medications or substances that could affect your ability to understand the MSA or the previous negotiations leading to your agreements,
- whether you have reviewed the MSA,
- whether you have any questions about the MSA,
- whether the MSA fully resolves all of the issues between you and your spouse, including custody, support, and the division of assets, and
- whether you think the MSA is fair and reasonable;

Questions to verify that you understand the consequences of the MSA, such as:
- whether you know that you could proceed to trial instead of entering into a settlement agreement,

- whether you understand that a trial could generate results either more or less favorable to you than your MSA, and
- whether you understand that once the judge accepts the MSA and makes it a part of your divorce judgment, you will have permanently waived your right to a trial;

Questions to verify that you are entering into the MSA voluntarily, such as:
- whether you believe that anyone is forcing you to enter into the MSA, and
- whether you wish the court to accept the MSA and make it part of your divorce judgment.

The court will not examine the fairness of the MSA and will not change any of the terms. You must be sure that you are satisfied with the MSA before attending the hearing. At the conclusion of the hearing, the judge will sign your final judgment of divorce and your marriage will be legally dissolved.

> "The hard work has been done, so the uncontested divorce hearing is just a formality."

Bari Z. Weinberger, Esq.

A Note About Potential Post-Judgment Matters: Modifying or Enforcing Orders and Agreements

For many fortunate people, entry of a final divorce decree means that everything connected with the former marriage has been settled once and for all. This is more likely to be the case for couples who have reached agreement on all of their issues and proceeded through an uncontested divorce. Even in that case, however, there are sometimes matters that arise after a final judgment of divorce that require the former spouses to engage in additional settlement negotiations or even appear in court.

The majority of disputes that arise post-divorce occur when:
- one party fails to carry out the orders of the court, or
- a change of circumstances justifies a modification of the court's orders.

Fortunately, enforcement matters rarely come up for parties who have entered into settlement agreements, although it is not unheard of for one spouse to refuse to comply with the terms of an MSA or for disputes to develop regarding what certain terms mean. (This is one reason it is so important to have attorney assistance during the process.) If you have included a provision in your settlement agreement requiring mediation of any enforcement disputes, that will be your first step. If you find yourself facing a need for court interventions over a dispute, you can file a "motion to enforce litigant's rights."

As previously noted, you and your spouse can modify your MSA in the future by mutual agreement and file the amended agreement with the court. If you have a disagreement about whether or not a modification is necessary, and you are unable to resolve it out of court, you can file a motion for modification.

Information on procedures for filing post-judgment motions in New Jersey family court are available directly from the court. It is highly advisable to have attorney assistance with any such a motion. Motions for modification or enforcement must be brought promptly to avoid losing the right to do so due to statutes of limitations and other factors.

- - - - -

Further Information and Resources:

- Weinberger Divorce & Family Law Group maintains a listing of all New Jersey courthouses on the website: http://bit.ly/nj-courts, including directions and contact information as well as additional helpful information relating to each individual New Jersey county.

- The Court Rules governing practice in New Jersey state courts can be found at the New Jersey Courts official website: http://bit.ly/courtrulesNJ. NJRules specific to family law appear in Part V. The general rules in Part I also apply to family law cases. The rules governing civil actions in general appear in Part IV and apply to civil family law cases unless a more specific rule appears in Part V. You can find more specific information in the Rules themselves.

- For more information about the Case Information Statement and how it is used in the New Jersey divorce process, see "New Jersey Case Information Statement Explained," by Bari Z. Weinberger, Esq. on the Weinberger Divorce & Family Law Group website: http://bit.ly/divorce-cis.

- Legal Services of New Jersey (LSNJ) maintains a statewide legal hotline providing brief telephone advice, attorney referrals pertaining to civil law matters, and additional attorney assistance for low income and other vulnerable populations. Both English and Spanish speaking attorneys are available. You can contact LSNJ toll free at (888) LSNJ-LAW or via the Legal Services of New Jersey official website: http://bit.ly/LegalSNJ.

- The Servicemembers Civil Relief Act (SCRA) is contained in Title 50 of the United States Code (50 U.S.C. App Section 501 et seq.). Rules regarding default judgments and stays of proceedings are found at sections 521 and 522 on the Department of Justice official website: http://bit.ly/military-scra.

- For more information specific to military families, including two PowerPoint presentations providing an introduction to military divorce in New Jersey and an overview of rights and responsibilities of military parents in New Jersey, see "Military Divorce: New Jersey Divorce When You or Your Spouse is in the Military" at: http://bit.ly/military-guide.

What to Bring To An Initial Consultation

When meeting with an attorney for the first time, it is essential to bring as many of the following items as possible:

Financial Information
(including account names, numbers, balances and current statements)
- ☐ Individual and business income tax returns for the past 3-5 years (state and federal)
- ☐ W-2 statements for the past 3-5 years for both parties
- ☐ Recent employment pay stubs (3) for both parties
- ☐ Bank statements (monthly) for the past 1-3 years for joining and individual accounts
- ☐ Stock, bond and mutual fund monthly account statements for the past 1-3 years
- ☐ Account statement for annuities, CDs, 529s, UTMA/UGMA, etc. for the past 1-3 years
- ☐ Social Security statement for both parties

Retirement Savings Information
(including balances, beneficiaries, outstanding loans and account statements)
- ☐ 401(k)s and 403(b)s
- ☐ IRAs
- ☐ SERPs, SEPs, Keoughs, etc.
- ☐ Pension statements

Property Information
(including property description, address, ownership interest, market value, outstanding mortgage and loan balances, source of mortgage and loan payments and most recent tax assessment)

- ☐ Primary residence
- ☐ Rental properties (including any rental income)
- ☐ Vacation homes and time shares
- ☐ Business property (what percentage ownership is allocated to you)
- ☐ Personal property of value (antiques, collectables, jewelry, art, furs, etc.)
- ☐ Inheritance (past, current or anticipated)
- ☐ Interests in a trust (current or future)
- ☐ List of property owned by each party prior to marriage
- ☐ Vehicles, boats, motorcycles, etc.
- ☐ List of safety deposit box contents with a photocopy of signature cards
- ☐ Gifts to individual

Child Related Expenses
- ☐ Number and ages of children
- ☐ Health insurance
- ☐ Medical expenses
- ☐ Education (general expenses, savings accounts, or other)
- ☐ Gifts or transfers to minors (UGMA/UTMA)
- ☐ Special needs (education plan, medical needs, associated costs or other)

Bills and Outstanding Debt
(including balances, statements, source of payments, funds)
- ☐ Credit card statements whether joint or individual for 1-3 years
- ☐ Loan documents
- ☐ Leases on vehicles
- ☐ Tax liens / debts due to the IRS

- ☐ Utility bills for the past 1-3 months
- ☐ Money due to third parties on Notes Payable
- ☐ Student loans / tuition, etc.
- ☐ Outstanding medical bills
- ☐ Arrears on prior support orders and agreements (child support / alimony)
- ☐ Monthly budget worksheet (Quick Books, Quicken, Case Information Statement)

Legal Agreements
- ☐ Wills
- ☐ Living wills
- ☐ Powers of attorney
- ☐ Advance healthcare directive, healthcare
- ☐ Pre-nuptial agreement, post-nuptial agreement
- ☐ Divorce judgments / agreements or child support orders from a previous marriage
- ☐ Business partnership agreements, records, books

Insurance Documents and Information
(including statements where available)
- ☐ Health Insurances: carrier name, policy and group numbers, persons covered
- ☐ Life Insurances: carrier name, policy number, face amount, cash value, insured, and beneficiaries
- ☐ Auto Insurance: carrier name, policy number, vehicles covered, insured, term period
- ☐ Homeowner's Insurance: carrier name, policy number, residence covered
- ☐ Long Term Care Insurance: carrier name, policy number, insured
- ☐ Disability Insurance: carrier name, policy number, insured

5 Overlooked Factors That Can Wreak Havoc on Your Finances

1. **Case Information Statement:**
   Lack of a comprehensive CIS can adversely affect the outcome of any future litigation. For example, if your financial situation changes later, such as through a job loss, small overlooked details in your CIS can significantly harm your chances of getting any relief.

2. **Tax Consequences:**
   Certain disbursement arrangements can add unexpected tax burdens. Retirement accounts are one example. If the tax liability isn't accurately factored in your settlement, it can be worth a lot less than you thought it would be.

3. **Being Unprepared:**
   A lawyer will need numerous documents from you: bank statements, records of debt, tax returns...And they bill by the hour...Failing to gather and organize the right documents yourself means you will end up paying your lawyer hundreds per hour just to do administrative tasks.

4. **Overlooked Assets:**
   Inexperienced attorneys and those representing themselves often overlook non-material assets. Items such as frequent flyer miles and reward points have value. Non-material assets can be used as a bargaining chip, even if they aren't important to you.

5. **Underestimating Asset Value:**
   One example is the value of household contents. Furniture, artwork, tools, coin collections, memorabilia, all have value that should be calculated and could be significant.

5 Overlooked Factors That Can Wreak Havoc on Your Parenting

1. **Visitation:**
   Small items, like specific pickup / drop-off times, can cause never-ending frustration. Do you want your former spouse to be able to show up unannounced, drop the children off after their bedtime or interfere with your personal plans?

2. **Education:**
   Private school and college costs are often not addressed when children are young at the time of divorce. Post judgment litigation to address the issue later can cost thousands. If these issues are not addressed prior to divorce, your child's first year tuition may be spent on litigation rather than education.

3. **Shared Custody:**
   Many parents misunderstand how this works and how much autonomy they lose. The level of ongoing interaction required severely limits your options, meaning greater restrictions on your mobility and decision-making.

4. **Emancipation:**
   A child **is not** automatically emancipated at age 18. This mistake has actually led to incarceration when a parent failed to pay child support while their child was is in college. Not every case is the same so make sure you address this issue with your attorney.

5. **Unexpected 'Agreements'**:
   Making an *'exception'* to the terms of your agreement or going along with an informal plan that you expect to be short term can come back to haunt you. The other parent can use this situation to get the court to make this a permanent modification.

5 Overlooked Factors That Can Wreak Havoc on Your Future

1. **Life Insurance:**
   Not adequately insuring the divorce settlement can leave you destitute if your former spouse passes away. Alimony *terminates* upon death. You would have no recourse against the estate for years of alimony you were counting on. Protect yourself by incorporating life insurance into your divorce agreement.

2. **Debt:**
   Improper handling of marital debt can cause present and future financial problems. Financial burden and collection calls can become a daily stressor when debt is overlooked. Your credit rating can suffer. Bankruptcy is unfortunately a common outcome due to poor handling of marital debt.

3. **Inaccurate Information:**
   If you hide information from your lawyer - or your lawyer doesn't ask you for the right information - you could leave yourself open to serious sanctions from the court. The court may view you as untrustworthy and side with your spouse.

4. **Time**:
   Allowing too much time to pass before enforcing a court order can leave you without recourse. For example, if your ex fails to pay for unreimbursed medical expenses, allowing too much time to go by before seeking enforcement could leave you unable to collect.

5. **Documentation**:
    Paying with cash vs. leaving a paper trail is a common error. If you can't prove that you've made a cash payment, you may be required to pay again. Failure to keep receipts can create a proof problem, thus preventing you from collecting a reimbursement. Losing or misplacing your divorce agreement often leads to unintentional non-compliance and sanctions.

For More Information

At Weinberger Divorce & Family Law Group all of our attorneys are engaged full time in the practice of family law. We are committed to providing honest recommendations and keeping the best interests of our clients and their children at the forefront at all times. Our attorneys will strive to resolve your matter out of court and will explore your settlement options, including New Jersey divorce mediation if appropriate in your case. When necessary, we will also fight vigorously to protect your rights.

You can find out more about our dedicated family law attorneys on our website, which is located at: www.WeinbergerLawGroup.com. Weinberger Divorce & Family Law Group offers an initial consultation with an experienced New Jersey Family Law Attorney at no cost.

Weinberger Divorce & Family Law Group has offices located throughout New Jersey.

Weinberger Divorce & Family Law Group Headquarter Offices:
119 Cherry Hill Road, Suite 120
Parsippany, NJ 07054
Morris County

Tel: (888) 888-0919

Weinberger Divorce & Family Law Group
Safeguarding Your Future™

Other Book Titles:
Weinberger Law Group Library Series of Family Law Guides

Contested Divorce

Child Support

Child Custody

Alimony

Property Division

eBook and/or print versions of the Weinberger Law Group Library series can be ordered via Amazon or by visiting www.WeinbergerLawGroup.com.

Made in the USA
Middletown, DE
26 August 2020